Welcome!

All of the ingredients in this book are safe to use,
but make sure you always follow these rules...

Before You Start

* Read the instructions before starting, and follow them carefully.

* Gather all the ingredients and equipment before you start.

* Don't use any ingredients not listed in the recipes, and make sure an adult has checked them over before you start sliming.

* Any slime making should be done under adult supervision. We've highlighted times when a grown-up should do something for you.

* No snacking around the slime-making area, and when we say slimes cannot be eaten—we mean it!

* Keep children under 3 years old and all animals away from your slime experiments.

* Wear eye protection, and keep slimy hands away from your eyes.

* Only make and play with slime on hard surfaces—keep away from furniture, carpets, and other delicate items that are hard to clean.

* Always store your slime in an airtight container (see p64) and place in the fridge. Throw it away after a week. Some slimes will need to be thrown away immediately after play—check the recipe instructions carefully.

* Watch out when using paint or food colouring—it can stain. Wear rubber gloves so you don't stain your hands.

* Always wash your hands before and after making and playing with slime.

* Clean up after yourself! Wash all equipment and surfaces (see p64).

* A lot of the slimes use saline solution. Make sure you use this and not lens cleaner or contact lens solution.

* Don't throw your slimes down the sink or toilet after you've finished with them—throw them in the trash.

SUPER SLIME

DK

Editor Sophie Parkes
US senior editor Allison Singer
Jacket designer Elle Ward
Pre-production producer
Dragana Puvacic
Senior producer Amy Knight
Managing art editor Gemma Glover
Creative director Helen Senior
Publisher Sarah Larter

Written, designed, edited, and
project-managed for DK by Dynamo Ltd.

First American Edition, 2019
Published in the United States by DK Publishing
1450 Broadway, Suite 801, New York, NY 10018

A catalog record for this book
is available from the Library of Congress.
ISBN: 978-1-4654-8571-7

DK books are available at special discounts when
purchased in bulk for sales promotions, premiums,
fund-raising, or educational use. For details, contact:
DK Publishing Special Markets, 1450 Broadway,
Suite 801, New York, NY 10018
SpecialSales@dk.com

Printed and bound in China

A WORLD OF IDEAS:
SEE ALL THERE IS TO KNOW

www.dk.com

The publisher would like to thank the following people for
their help in photographing, making, and handling slime:
Mia Pestridge, Leo Sandford, and Kate Ford.

All photography © Tim Pestridge/DK

Welcome!

Slime fun is waiting just over the page,
but remember:

* None of the recipes in this book are edible—
DO NOT eat them.
* All recipes containing food must be thrown
away on the day you play with them. Take
extra care when handling raw egg.
* Always wash your hands thoroughly before
and after handling slime.
* All of our recipes use biodegradable glitter.

Contents

Basic Slime Kit

Most of the recipes in this book need the following items...

bowls

measuring spoons

clear craft glue   PVA glue

mixing spoon or spatula

cornstarch   saline solution   baking soda   shaving cream

Here are some of the extras you'll need. Check each recipe for specific ingredients.

buttons

plastic beads, gems, and pompoms

liquid dish soap

felt-tip markers

biodegradable glitter

shimmer dust

Most ingredients in this book are easy to find, but if you can't get certain items, ask an adult to buy them or order them online.

Play Dough Slime

If you're new to slime, this is a great recipe to get you started. With only a few ingredients, it's super easy and fun!

YOU WILL NEED

* 1 cup hair conditioner
* 5 drops of food coloring
* 4 cups cornstarch

Squeeze the hair conditioner into a mixing bowl and stir in the food coloring.

Mix in the cornstarch. If the mixture is still wet, add in more cornstarch gradually and keep mixing as you go!

Knead and squish the slime with your hands until it feels like dough.

SCIENCE BIT!

Do you want to know why we add cornstarch? It helps bind and thicken mixtures. As well as being used for slime, cornstarch can be used in pudding, gravy, and lots of other sauces.

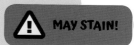

⚠ MAY STAIN!

Butter Slime

This slime can be spread with a knife, just like butter! It's so good you'll want to share the recipe with all your friends.

YOU WILL NEED

* 1 cup PVA glue
* 1 tsp baking soda
* 3 tbsp water
* 2–3 drops food coloring
* 1 tsp baby oil
* 2 tbsp baby lotion
* 1 tbsp saline solution—it must contain boric acid and sodium borate
* 2–4 tbsp cornstarch

1

Pour the PVA glue into a bowl and mix in the baking soda and water. Then stir in your food coloring.

TIME:
10 MINUTES

DIFFICULTY:
EASY

WARNING:
NONEDIBLE

 ⚠ **MAY STAIN!**

2

Mix in the baby oil and baby lotion. Next, beat in the saline solution.

The mixture will probably still be sticky, so add the cornstarch and stir until you can start to knead it with your hands. The more you knead, the less sticky it will become!

3

Toothpaste Slime

Do you want a slime that smells minty fresh? This is the recipe for you!

YOU WILL NEED

* About 4 tubes (16 oz/450 g total) of toothpaste
* baby lotion
* 1¼ cup cornstarch
* baby oil

1

Squeeze the toothpaste into a microwave-safe bowl and heat for 16 minutes, getting an adult to stir it regularly. Be careful, as it gets very hot! Leave this to cool for two hours.

MAY STAIN!

When cool, stir in baby lotion, just a little at a time, to make a smooth texture. Then, add the cornstarch until the mixture becomes crumbly.

2

3

Gradually add drops of baby oil until the slime texture becomes smooth. Be careful not to make it too oily!

TIME:
2 HOURS, 10 MINS

· · · · · · · · · · · · · · · · · · ·

DIFFICULTY:
INTERMEDIATE

· · · · · · · · · · · · · · · · · · ·

WARNING:
NONEDIBLE

TOP TIP!
· · · · · · · · · · · · ·

Ask an adult to stir the toothpaste regularly while it is in the microwave. This stops it from burning or sticking to the bowl.

Egg-cellent Slime

Are you ready to take your slime to the egg-streme? Here's all you need to know.

YOU WILL NEED

* 2 egg whites
* 4 tbsp liquid dish soap
* glitter

2

Mix in the liquid dish soap really well, then pop your slime in the fridge overnight (for at least eight hours) to set. If it's still runny, leave it for a few more hours.

1

Ask an adult to help you separate the egg whites from the yolks into a mixing bowl.

TIME:
OVERNIGHT

DIFFICULTY:
EASY

WARNING:
NONEDIBLE

3

SAFETY FIRST

Always wash your hands well after handling this slime because it contains raw egg. Don't keep this slime for more than 24 hours.

Your slime should now feel squishy. It's time to add some glitter and start playing with your creation.

MAY STAIN!

Slime Stress Balls

Make some clear slime and squeeze it into balloons to make your own stress balls!

YOU WILL NEED

FOR THE CLEAR SLIME

* ½ tsp baking soda
* ½ cup warm water
* ⅔ cup clear craft glue
* Saline solution—it must contain boric acid and sodium borate

FOR THE STRESS BALL

* balloons
* fruit or vegetable net bag

TIME:
10 MINUTES

DIFFICULTY:
EASY

WARNING:
NONEDIBLE

Put the baking soda and water into a bowl and mix in the clear glue.

Beat in small amounts of saline solution until the mixture turns gloopy. Add more if it is too sticky!

3

Push your clear slime mix into a balloon and tie up the end.

4

Wrap the net bag around the balloon. Enjoy squishing and squeezing your stress ball.

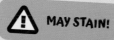 MAY STAIN!

TOP TIP!

Be careful not to overfill your balloon and make sure there are no big air bubbles inside before you tie it up.

Draw-on Slime

It's time to get artsy! Make this stretchy white slime that you can doodle all over with your markers.

YOU WILL NEED

* 1 tsp baking soda
* 1 cup PVA glue
* 1 tbsp saline solution—it must contain boric acid and sodium borate
* felt-tip markers

2

Next, stir in the saline solution. The slime should start to get stringy and come away from the edge of the bowl.

1

Pour the baking soda and glue into a bowl and mix them together well.

3

Now it's time to start kneading and squishing the slime with your hands.

4

The slime should feel rubbery. Stretch out your slime and get drawing!

TIME:
10 MINUTES

DIFFICULTY:
EASY

WARNING:
NONEDIBLE

15

Color Combo Slime

TIME:
10 MINUTES

DIFFICULTY:
EASY

WARNING:
NONEDIBLE

This recipe shows you how to turn clear slime into colorful swirls!

YOU WILL NEED

* clear slime ingredients (see pages 12–13)
* pink and yellow food coloring
* pink and yellow biodegradable glitter

1

Make your clear slime, then divide it into two bowls. Add pink food coloring to one half and yellow to the other.

⚠ MAY STAIN!

TOP TIP!

You can try all kinds of colors to invent your own super slime. How about blue-and-green ocean slime? Have fun experimenting!

2

Sprinkle lots of glitter onto each slime color to make it shimmer. Use your hands to mix it together.

3

Lay your two slimes out into strips and mix the two colors together to make awesome swirls.

17

Avalanche Slime

Turn over your bowl of avalanche slime to watch it blend into magical colors!

YOU WILL NEED

* clear slime ingredients (see pages 12–13)
* stretchy slime ingredients (see pages 14–15)
* food coloring (try yellow and green)
* biodegradable glitter

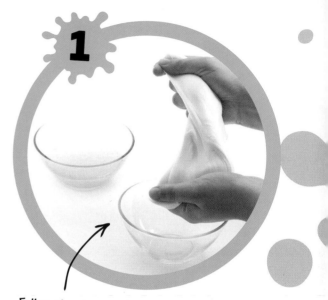

1

Follow the steps on pages 12–13 to make the clear slime, and pages 14–15 for the stretchy slime.

2

Split the clear slime in half and make each half a different color using glitter and food coloring.

3

Put the two colors of slime into a bowl together and spread some stretchy slime on top.

TIME:
40 MINUTES

DIFFICULTY:
EASY

WARNING:
NONEDIBLE

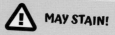 **MAY STAIN!**

Look at how
the white slime
blends with the
other colors!

4

Leave the slime
to settle for about
half an hour.

5

Now tip it out onto a plate
and watch the avalanche!

19

Galaxy Slime

This galaxy slime is out of this world!

YOU WILL NEED

* clear slime ingredients (see pages 12–13)
* pink, blue, black, and red food coloring
* glitter

1

Make clear slime using the recipe on pages 12–13. Now split your slime into four bowls and make each a different color.

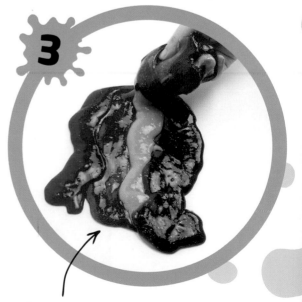

2

Add lots of glitter to each color. It works best if you mix it in with your hands.

3

Lay out all the slimes and start twisting the colors together!

TIME:
10 MINUTES

DIFFICULTY:
EASY

WARNING:
NONEDIBLE

TOP TIP!

Try adding star-shaped
sequins to your slime
for a cosmic effect!

Fish in a Bag

With some toy fish and a freezer bag, you can transform blue slime into one of these incredible creations!

YOU WILL NEED

* clear slime ingredients (see pages 12–13)
* blue finger paint
* ribbon
* freezer bag (with no holes!)
* plastic toy fish

1

Make clear slime using the recipe on pages 12–13, and mix in a blob of blue paint.

2

Pop some colorful toy fish into your slime.

3

Put your slime into a freezer bag and secure the top with a piece of ribbon.

This slime would make a great gift for your friends.

TOP TIP!

Try adding glitter or sequins to make shimmering water.

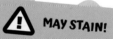

⚠ **MAY STAIN!**

23

Candy Cane

Want to combine stretchy slime with clear slime in a cool way? Here's an idea for how to do just that.

YOU WILL NEED

* clear slime (see pages 12–13)
* stretchy slime (see pages 14–15)
* red glitter
* red food coloring

1

Make a bowl of clear slime (see pages 12–13).

2

Mix up some stretchy slime (see pages 14–15).

Lay the two slimes out in strips and use your hands to twist them together into stripes.

TOP TIP!

. . . .

You can make striped colors in any combination you like. How about twisting together three colors?

4

3

Add red food coloring and glitter to the clear slime and mix it in.

TIME:
15 MINUTES
. . . .

DIFFICULTY:
EASY
. . . .

WARNING:
NONEDIBLE

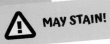
⚠ MAY STAIN!

Melted Snowman

This stretchy slime recipe is perfect for wintertime fun. Why stop at one snowman? You could make a whole family!

YOU WILL NEED

* 1 cup PVA glue
* 1 tsp baking soda
* 1 tbsp saline solution—it must contain boric acid and sodium borate
* buttons, pompoms, and a triangle of orange construction paper to decorate

TIME:
10 MINUTES

DIFFICULTY:
EASY

WARNING:
NONEDIBLE

2

Beat in the saline solution until the slime starts to get stringy. Knead the mix with your hands. You should be able to pick it up without it sticking to you!

1

Pour the glue and baking soda into your bowl and mix together well.

3

Stretch out your slime and put the button eyes, carrot nose, and pompom smile in place. Your slime should look like a snowman that has melted across the table.

MAY STAIN!

Mash-up Slime

What happens when you bring together fluffy and clear slime? This mind-boggling mash-up, that's what!

YOU WILL NEED

FOR THE FLUFFY SLIME

* 2¼ cups shaving cream (not gel)
* food coloring of your choice
* ¼ cup PVA glue
* ¼ tsp of baking soda
* 1 tbsp saline solution—it must contain boric acid and sodium borate
* small Styrofoam balls

FOR THE CLEAR SLIME

* clear slime (see pages 12–13)
* glitter and sequins
* food coloring of your choice

1

Mix the shaving cream with a couple of drops of food coloring, then stir in the glue and baking soda.

2

Next, whip in the saline solution until the mixture comes together, and fold in some Styrofoam balls.

TIME:
15 MINUTES

DIFFICULTY:
EASY

WARNING:
NONEDIBLE

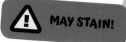

⚠ **MAY STAIN!**

3

Make up some clear slime (page 12–13) and add food coloring, glitter, and sequins.

4

Finally, mix the two slimes together and start playing!

TOP TIP!

This recipe works best if you make your fluffy slime a different color than your clear slime. Having two different textures is what makes this slime so fun to handle!

Festive Slime

TIME:
5 MINUTES

DIFFICULTY:
EASY

WARNING:
NONEDIBLE

This recipe is great for when you're feeling festive. Have fun decorating your slime with lots of colorful glitter and sequins!

YOU WILL NEED

* ½ tsp baking soda
* ½ cup warm water
* ¾ cup clear craft glue
* green food coloring
* saline solution—it must contain boric acid and sodium borate
* glitter, pompoms, and sequins

1

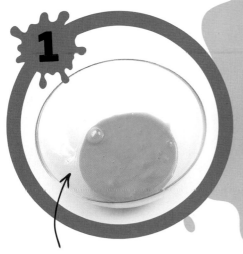

Mix the baking soda and water together with the clear glue and green food coloring.

2

Stir in small amounts of saline solution until the slime starts to form. Then get your hands involved!

3

Lay out the slime and get crafty by sprinkling glitter and sequins on top.

TOP TIP!

. . . .

Go one step further and add a handful of pompoms to your festive slime. The more colors the better!

⚠ **MAY STAIN!**

Rubber Band Slime

This is an awesome way to play with any extra rubber bands or loom bands.

YOU WILL NEED

* clear slime ingredients (see pages 12–13)
* rubber bands or loom bands
* glitter
* sequins

1

First, make clear slime using the recipe and steps on pages 12–13.

2

Sprinkle in some glitter and sequins. Use your hands to mix them in well.

TIME:
10 MINUTES

DIFFICULTY:
EASY

WARNING:
NONEDIBLE

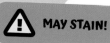 **MAY STAIN!**

TOP TIP!
. . . .

Try adding food coloring,
or putting different fun
things in the slime—pom poms
or super chunky glitter work
really well.

3

Finally, add in a handful
of colorful rubber or loom bands,
mix, and your slime is ready!

Scented Slime

This slime smells so good you'll never want to put it down—but don't add too much peppermint or it might smell too strong!

YOU WILL NEED

* clear slime ingredients (see pages 12–13)
* red food coloring
* gold glitter
* 1 tsp peppermint essence

1

Make some clear slime using the recipe on pages 12–13 and stir in some food coloring.

⚠ MAY STAIN!

TIME:
5 MINUTES

DIFFICULTY:
EASY

WARNING:
NONEDIBLE

Finally, add in a drop of peppermint essence and mix it in well.

3

Sprinkle in as much gold glitter as you like.

2

TOP TIP!

If you like adding a scent to your slime, you could try experimenting with different ones. How about vanilla extract? Although these slimes smell delicious, don't eat them!

Fake Vomit

TIME:
10 MINUTES

DIFFICULTY:
EASY

WARNING:
NONEDIBLE

WARNING: Things are about to get totally gross! This fake vomit is sure to make your friends and family squirm. So, bring on the yuck!

YOU WILL NEED

* ½ tsp baking soda
* ½ cup warm water
* ¾ cup clear craft glue
* saline solution—it must contain boric acid and sodium borate
* lentils
* yellow and brown food coloring

1

Mix the baking soda and water together in a bowl.

2

Add in the clear glue, and stir in a little saline solution at a time until a gloopy slime starts to form.

3

Squirt in a few drops of food coloring, then use your hands to squish in some lentils.

SAFETY FIRST

This slime doesn't last for long. Play with it, then throw it away on the day you make it. Only make slime on a surface that can be wiped down, and never play with it near carpets—it can stain and damage furniture. Always ask a grown-up to help you.

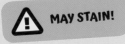 MAY STAIN!

Radioactive Slime

Grab some luminous green food coloring to bring this bubbling recipe to life.

YOU WILL NEED

* ½ cup warm water
* ½ tsp baking soda
* ¾ cup clear craft glue
* saline solution—it must contain boric acid and sodium borate
* lime green food coloring

1 Put your water and baking soda into a bowl and mix in the clear glue.

2 Gradually drop in the saline solution and stir well, until the mixture turns gloopy. Add a drop or two of food coloring until you get the radioactive look you want!

3

TIME:
5 MINUTES
....

DIFFICULTY:
EASY
....

WARNING:
NONEDIBLE

Beat the mixture with
a spoon or spatula until
your slime is thick enough
to be handled.

Dish Soap Slime

This recipe proves that liquid dish soap can be fun!

YOU WILL NEED

* 2 tbsp liquid dish soap
* 2 tbsp clear glue
* ½ tsp saline solution—it must contain boric acid and sodium borate
* glitter

TIME:
5 MINUTES

DIFFICULTY:
EASY

WARNING:
NONEDIBLE

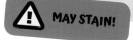 **MAY STAIN!**

1

Mix together the liquid dish soap and clear glue.

Slowly drop in the saline solution.
Stir until the slime begins to form.

2

3

Finally, add in some glitter.
Your slime is ready to play with!

Color-changing Slime

Sunshine is all you need to turn this snazzy slime ALL the colors!

YOU WILL NEED

* ½ tsp baking soda
* ½ cup warm water
* ¾ cup clear craft glue
* saline solution—it must contain boric acid and sodium borate
* UV color-changing beads

Add the glue, then stir in small amounts of saline solution until the slime begins to form a clear ball with bubbles inside.

2

1

Mix together the baking soda and water in your bowl.

⚠ MAY STAIN!

TIME:
10 MINUTES

DIFFICULTY:
EASY

WARNING:
NONEDIBLE

TOP TIP!
· · · · · · · · · · · ·

Put your UV color-changing beads in the sunlight to charge them up first. This will help them show up better when they're added to the slime.

When it's all mixed in, see how the beads change color outside on a sunny day.

3

4

INSIDE!

OUTSIDE!

Next, pour in your UV color-changing beads.

Marbled Silver Slime

Follow these simple steps to find out how to create a shimmery, shiny slime marbled with silver.

YOU WILL NEED

* clear slime ingredients (see pages 12–13)
* blue shimmer dust or food coloring
* silver glitter

1

Make clear slime using the recipe on pages 12–13, then split it into two. Make one blob a bit bigger than the other. Add lots of silver glitter to the bigger bit!

2

Add blue shimmer dust to the smaller bit.

3

Carefully use your hands to blend the two colors.

MAY STAIN!

TIME:
10 MINUTES

DIFFICULTY:
EASY

WARNING:
NONEDIBLE

SCIENCE BIT!
· · · · · · · · · · · · · · · ·
All slime recipes need activating
ingredients to make them work. These
slime **activators** help turn glue into slime.
Here the activator is saline solution, which
chemically bonds with the glue when you mix it.

45

Halloween Slime

If you like everything spooky, you'll love this glow-in-the-dark slime!

YOU WILL NEED

* ½ tsp baking soda
* ½ cup warm water
* ¾ cup clear craft glue
* saline solution—it must contain boric acid and sodium borate
* glow-in-the-dark finger paint
* toy spiders

Beat the mixture until your slime stops sticking to the bowl.

Mix together the baking soda, water, and glue. Add a dollop of glow-in-the-dark paint and stir in the saline solution a little at a time.

Add the toy spiders and switch off the lights to see the results! Don't forget to wash your hands when you've finished playing.

⚠ MAY STAIN!

3

TIME:
10 MINUTES

DIFFICULTY:
EASY

WARNING:
NONEDIBLE

TOP TIP!
. . . .
Charge up your slime under a lamp or in natural daylight. Then it'll be ready to glow bright after dark!

Springtime Slime

Transform a bowl of clear slime into something sparkly and full of flowers. Just follow these simple instructions!

YOU WILL NEED

* ½ cup warm water
* ½ tsp baking soda
* ¾ cup clear craft glue
* saline solution—it must contain boric acid and sodium borate
* flower confetti or floral decorations
* glitter

1

Mix the water and baking soda in your bowl.

TIME:
10 MINUTES

DIFFICULTY:
EASY

WARNING:
NONEDIBLE

⚠ MAY STAIN!

2

Stir in the clear glue. Add small amounts of saline solution until the slime mixture gloops together. Then mix in the glitter.

3

Sprinkle lots of flower confetti or floral decorations to complete your springtime slime!

SCIENCE BIT!

. . . .

Glue is made up of groups of atoms called polymers. When you mix it with saline solution the polymers stick together, turning the glue from a liquid into a solid.

Fake Ice-cream Slime

Whip up this fake ice-cream slime in your fantasy ice-cream factory. Get creative adding sprinkles and toppings—but don't eat it!

YOU WILL NEED

* 2 tsp baking soda
* ¼ cup boiling water
* 1 cup clear glue
* ⅓ cup cold water
* 1 tsp saline solution—it must contain boric acid and sodium borate
* 1¼ cup shaving cream
* plastic ice-cream cones
* sprinkles

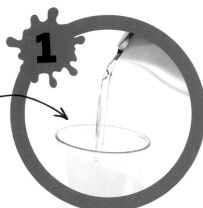

1 Put the baking soda into a jug, then very carefully pour in the boiling water and mix together. Leave this to cool.

In a separate bowl, mix the glue with the cold water and stir in the saline solution.

2

Then combine the two mixtures and leave to rest for half an hour.

TIME:
45 MINUTES

DIFFICULTY:
MODERATE

WARNING:
NONEDIBLE

SAFETY FIRST!

Always ask a grown-up to help you with boiling water.

3

Next, start folding in the shaving cream.

Top it off with colorful sprinkles!

4

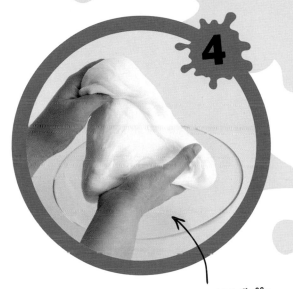

Use your hands to knead the slime until it's fluffy.
Add a little more shaving cream if needed.

TOP TIP!
. . . .

Try making a differently textured fake ice cream next! Check out this one, which we made using the fluffy slime recipe on page 28. What color fake ice cream will you make?

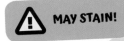

⚠ **MAY STAIN!**

Mad Scientist Slime

Get ready to try out this bubbly slime step-by-step.
Once the foaming stops, you'll be left with a great slime!

YOU WILL NEED

* ¼ cup distilled malt vinegar
* 1 tbs saline solution—it must contain boric acid and sodium borate
* ⅔ cup PVA glue
* food coloring
* a tray to put your foaming experiment on
* 1 tbsp baking soda

TIME:
15 MINUTES

DIFFICULTY:
INTERMEDIATE

WARNING:
NONEDIBLE

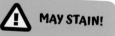 MAY STAIN!

1

First, pour the vinegar into a bowl. Stir in the saline solution and leave this to stand.

2

Add the PVA glue to a separate jug, drop in the food coloring, and give it a good mix. Put this onto a tray, then add the baking soda.

Take the vinegar and saline-solution mixture and pour it over the glue mixture. Quickly stir the mixture and watch as it starts to fizz up.

3

4

When the foaming stops, you'll be left with slime. Splash in a drop more saline solution if it's still too sticky to handle!

SCIENCE BIT!

When vinegar and baking soda mix together, they react to form carbon dioxide bubbles. These bubbles increase the pressure inside the jug, and the bubbles start overflowing out of the top.

Banana Play Clay

Pick up that sad, forgotten banana from the fruit bowl and turn it into slime!

YOU WILL NEED

* 1 ripe banana
* cornstarch
* 1 pinch of black fondant

SAFETY FIRST

This slime is NOT edible, and it can only be played with on the day that you make it. Make sure you throw it away after play to avoid bad smells.

1

Mash up your banana in a bowl with a fork.

TIME:
5 MINUTES

DIFFICULTY:
EASY

WARNING:
NONEDIBLE

MAY STAIN!

2

Fold in some black fondant to turn the mixture gray.

Mix in cornstarch a teaspoon at a time until you can handle the slime without it falling apart.

3

Now it's time to go bananas with your play clay!

Ketchup Slime

Perfect on fries, perfect for slime. Who knew that ketchup had so many talents?

YOU WILL NEED

* about 2 tbsp tomato ketchup
* 2 drops olive oil
* cornstarch

SAFETY FIRST! ⚠️

You must NOT eat ketchup slime. It's also important to know that this slime doesn't last long! Play with it on the day you make it, then throw it away to avoid any bad smells.

2

Stir in a couple of drops of olive oil.

Simply squirt the tomato ketchup into a bowl.

1

3

Add the cornstarch gradually until the mixture becomes less sticky. Then mix it with your hands!

TOP TIP!
. . . .
This slime is all about experimenting and NOT for eating. It would taste terrible, so don't try it!

⚠️ **MAY STAIN!**

TIME:
5 MINUTES
. . . .
DIFFICULTY:
EASY
. . . .
WARNING:
NONEDIBLE

Glitter Master Class

Here's a master class for perfecting your glitter technique! We'll show you how to layer up different types of glitter for the snazziest slime around.

YOU WILL NEED

* clear slime ingredients (see pages 12–13)
* lots and lots of glitter in different styles, shapes, and sizes. Some finer shimmer dust and some chunkier versions work well together.

⚠ **MAY STAIN!**

1

Make clear slime using the steps on pages 12–13 and start mixing in fine green glitter.

TIME: **10 MINUTES**

DIFFICULTY: **EASY**

WARNING: **NONEDIBLE**

Look at these for color and sparkle inspiration.

Next, sprinkle different shades of green glitter into your slime and keep mixing it in. Don't be afraid to add a lot!

2

3

Next add chunkier glitter in similar colors. We've used blue and yellow star shapes!

TOP TIP!
. . . .
You can add glitter to any slime recipe you like, but it works best of all in the clear slime. Have fun experimenting for yourself to see which you prefer.

Underwater Slime

Fill glistening blue slime with seashell confetti for this underwater slime.

YOU WILL NEED

* ½ tsp baking soda
* ½ cup warm water
* ⅔ cup clear craft glue
* saline solution—it must contain boric acid and sodium borate
* seashell confetti
* sequins
* blue shimmer dust or food coloring

TIME:
10 MINUTES

DIFFICULTY:
EASY

WARNING:
NONEDIBLE

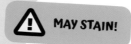
MAY STAIN!

Mix the baking soda with the water and glue.
Then sprinkle in the shimmer dust.

Add small amounts of saline solution until
the slime starts to gloop together.

3

Finally, add some sequins and colorful seashell confetti.

4

TOP TIP!
. . . .
If you don't have seashell confetti, you could add real shells or even little pebbles instead. Give it a try yourself!

Birthday Slime

This slime is ready to party. Pop it into party bags at your next birthday bash!

YOU WILL NEED

* clear slime ingredients (see pages 12–13)
* glitter
* balloon confetti

1

Make up a bowl of clear slime using the recipe on pages 12–13.

3

⚠ **MAY STAIN!**

Add another
color glitter.
(We used pink.)

2

Pour in lots of
your favorite
glitter color!

4

Then add in
your balloon
confetti.

63

Slime Storage

Look after your slime carefully to stop it from drying out. Make sure you store your slime in an airtight container in the fridge after play to keep it clean and slime-y. The slime may turn your container a different shade, so only use a tub that you're allowed to! Most slimes will last for up to a week, but some need to be thrown away right after play, so check the information in the recipes carefully.

A plastic box with a lid is perfect.

Cleaning Up

You won't be popular if you make a mess, so follow these rules for a happy slime-filled home:

* Always make slime on a wipe-clean surface.
* There's always a risk of staining with paint or food coloring, so it's best to lay down some newspaper first.
* Mop up any spillages as soon as you can.
* Wash up all bowls and spoons as soon as you've finished.
* Wipe down all surfaces and put your slime kit and ingredients away.
* NEVER pour slime failures down the sink or toilet—you'll block the drains! Put them in the trash.
* Always ask an adult before using cleaning products or liquid dish soap.

Hints and Tips

The recipes in this book should be easy to make, but slightly different ingredients may change the texture of the slime. With a bit of trial and error you should be able to get the results you want. Here are a few pointers:

 MY SLIME IS GETTING TOO HARD!
Slime doesn't last forever. Maybe it's time to make your next batch. What will you make this time?

 MY SLIME BREAKS WHEN I STRETCH IT!
Sounds like you've added too much saline solution. Try squirting a small amount of the glue you've used onto your slime and carefully fold it in.

 MY SLIME ISN'T GLITTERY ENOUGH!
If you're using PVA glue, make sure you've got a chunky glitter rather than a fine one or it will get lost. And remember the key rule when making a glittery slime—add some glitter, then add some more!

 MY GLUE-BASED SLIME IS TOO STICKY!
Add a few drops of saline solution and mix it in well.